CHANUKAH MUSIC FOR ALL HARPS

by SYLVIA WOODS

**each arranged for beginning
and advanced harp players**

This book is dedicated to Heidi Spiegel & Eve Gordon

Artwork by Heidi Spiegel

All arrangements by Sylvia Woods

Music Typeset by Sylvia Woods using the Music Printer Plus computer software

A companion cassette and a companion CD to this book are available from the Sylvia Woods Harp Center (see address below). On these recordings, Sylvia Woods plays all the pieces in this book and also in her 50 Christmas Carols For All Harps book. She plays them slower than they are usually played, so that you can play along while you're learning.

If you would like to receive a free catalog of books by Sylvia Woods and other books, recordings, harps, and accessories, please write to:
　　Sylvia Woods Harp Center
　　PO Box 816
　　Montrose, California 91021 USA
You can also find us on the Internet at www.harpcenter.com

© 1990 by Sylvia Woods, Woods Music & Books, Inc.
PO Box 816, Montrose CA 91021 USA

ISBN 0-936661-08-9

ALPHABETICAL INDEX OF TUNES

INTRODUCTION

Some of my proudest moments are when I get letters from harp players all over the world saying that they have played some of my arrangements for friends, or at a wedding, a party, or other occasion. I think it is wonderful that harp players can share their gift and their talents with others, and bring even more joy to festive days.

I have been asked by many harp players to write this book of music to play at Chanukah. Many of these letters have come from Jewish players who want to be able to share the Chanukah music with their family and friends. Others are from non-Jewish harp players who have received requests for Chanukah songs while playing at "Christmas Parties" or other December holiday parties. I am very happy to be able to provide this book for all of these players for the festive days of Chanukah.

I hope that you and your harp will put this book to good use. Get out there and share your beautiful music with the world! I'm proud of you all!

With much love,
Sylvia

ENGLISH TRANSLATIONS

Throughout this book whenever the English translations of the lyrics are written in regular type, they can be sung. *If the English words are printed in italics, the translation is loose, and does not fit with the music.*

MULTI-LEVEL BOOKS

This is the fourth book in the SYLVIA WOODS MULTI-LEVEL HARP BOOKS SERIES: books designed to be used by harpers and harpists of all levels of proficiency. Each tune has two arrangements: an easy version (A), and one that is more difficult (B). Also, each version contains chord indications that can be used by harp players or other instrumentalists.

Harp players can use this book many ways, depending on their purposes and abilitites. Here are a few suggestions.

1. A beginning player can play the melody alone, or with chords, or the complete easier arrangement.

2. More advanced players can play the easier arrangement, filling it out with more chords in the right or left hand, or play the second arrangement.

3. The easy arrangement can be played first, and then the harder arrangement, making a varied set.

4. The two arrangements can be played as a duet.

5. Additional instruments can be added to either arrangement, playing either the chords or the melody.

We hope you enjoy this book. If you'd like information on other books in this series, and other books by Sylvia Woods, please write to the Sylvia Woods Harp Center, P.O. Box 816, Montrose, CA 91021 USA and request our free mail order catalog.

Blessings Over The Candles
Chanukah Blessings

Slowly

Traditional

1. Baruch atah a-do-nai
E-lo-hey-nu melech ha-o-lam
A-sher kid'sha-nu b'mitz-vo-tav
V'tsi-va-nu l'chad leek ner,
Shel Chanukah.

2. Baruch atah a-do-nai
E-lo-hey-nu melech ha-o-lam
She-a-sa nee-sim la-vo-tay-nu
Ba-ya-mim ha-hem,
Baz-man ha-zeh.

3. Baruch atah a-do-nai
E-lo-hey-nu melech ha-o-lam
Sh'he chi-ya-nu, v'kee-ma-nu, v'hee-gee-ah-nu,
Laz'man ha-zeh.

Blessed art Thou, O Lord our God, King of the universe:
Who has commanded us to kindle the Chanukah light...
Who brought miracles to our ancestors so long ago...
Who hast given us in life and sustained us and brought us to
this season.....

Blessings Over The Candles
Chanukah Blessings

Slowly

Traditional

A Menorah is a candelabra which holds nine candles. Candles are lit for the eight days of Chanukah by the ninth candle called a Shammash*. The eight lights of the Menorah represent the jar of oil that continued to burn in the Temple in Jerusalem for eight days when it was thought to last only for one day. This traditional melody adapted for the blessings of the Menorah candles is sung each night of Chanukah. The third verse is only sung the first night.

*Shammash - A Hebrew word meaning Worker or Servant.

Chanukah, Chanukah

Playfully

Traditional

A folktune about how Chanukah is such a joyous holiday.

Chanukah, Chanukah, chag ya-fe kol kach.
Or cho-viv miso-viv, gil l'ye-led rach.
Chanukah, Chanukah, s'vivon sov, sov.
Sov sov sov, sov sov sov, mah no-im va-tov.

Chanukah is a merry holiday. Tops spin 'round, candles burn. Oh, let us sing and dance. Spin and turn while the candles burn...

Chanukah, Chanukah

Playfully

Traditional

7

Chanukah, O Chanukah

Folk harpers: if your harp does not have the low E (the last note of this piece), you can play it an octave higher.

With Spirit

Traditional

A popular song at Chanukah which began as a Yiddish poem. The tune, based on a Chassidic melody, became popularized by Klezmer, (Jewish traveling bands) who would play it during Chanukah. Originally sung in Yiddish it is more often heard today with the English text.

Chanukah, O Chanukah

Folk harpers: set the D# right above middle C before you begin. It will not need to be changed during the piece.
Pedal harpists: you will need to sharp the D pedal in measure 11, and natural it again at the end of the piece.

With Spirit

Traditional

Chanukah, O Chanukah come light the menorah
Let's have a party, we'll all dance the horah.
Gather 'round the table we'll give you a treat,
Sevivon to play with and latkes to eat. **
And while we are playing
The candles are burning low.
One for each night, they shed a sweet light

To remind us of days long ago,
One for each night, they shed a sweet light
To remind us of days long ago.

** Sevivon: A small spinning top, also called a dreydl.
Latkes: Potato pancakes.

Hanerot Halalu

Moderately

Traditional

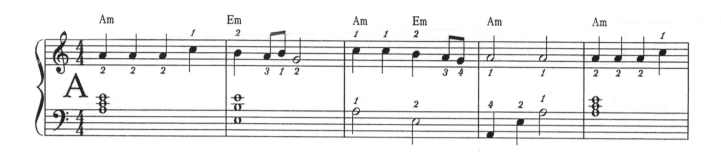

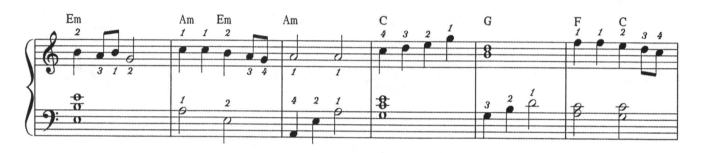

A Chassidic melody which usually is sung after the blessing of the candles.

Hanerot, hanerot, hanerot halalu,
Hanerot, hanerot, hanerot halalu.
Ah-nu maud-lee-keen, ah-nu maud-lee-keen,
Hanerot halalu, hanerot halalu.

These lights we do kindle...

Hanerot Halalu

Moderately

Traditional

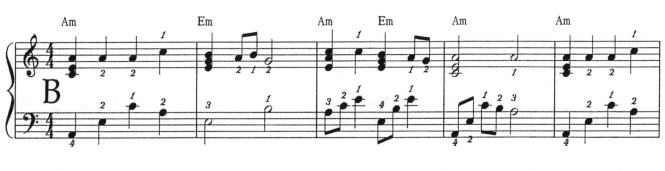

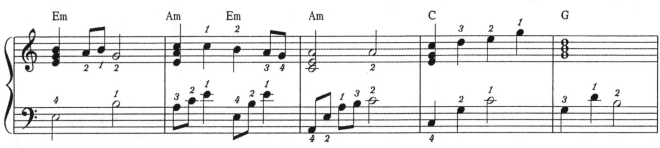

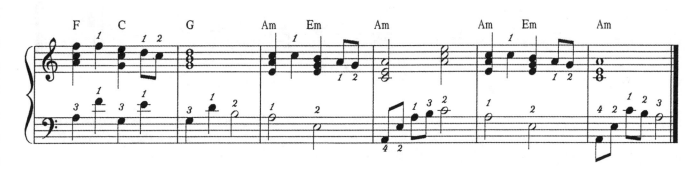

I Have A Little Dreydl
My Dreydl

Playfully

S.E. Goldfarb & S.S. Grossman

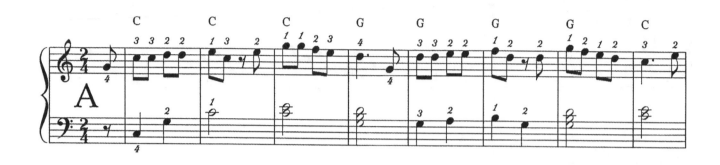

Playing Dreydls is a game of luck traditionally played during Chanukah. A dreydl is a small four-sided top. Inscribed on each side is a hebrew letter which directs the player what to do. Nun (N) means the player gets nothing from the pot, Gimmel (G), the player wins the whole pot, Heh (H), the player gets half and Shin (S), the player must add one to the pot.

1. I have a little dreydl,
I made it out of clay,
And when it's dry and ready
Then dreydl we shall play!
Oh dreydl, dreydl, dreydl,
I made it out of clay,
Oh dreydl, dreydl, dreydl,
Then dreydl we shall play!

2. It has a lovely body
With legs so short and thin,
And when it gets all tired
It drops and then I win!
Oh dreydl, dreydl, dreydl,
With legs so short and thin,
Oh dreydl, dreydl, dreydl,
It drops and then I win!

3. My dreydl's always playful,
It loves to dance and spin,
A happy game of dreydl
Come play, now let's begin!
Oh dreydl, dreydl, dreydl,
It loves to dance and spin,
Oh dreydl, dreydl, dreydl,
Come play, now let's begin!

©1950 by The United Synagogue of America. Utilized by permission.

I Have A Little Dreydl
My Dreydl

Playfully

S.E. Goldfarb & S.S. Grossman

Ma'oz Tsur
Rock of Ages

Majestically

Traditional

This song is one of the more traditional "hymns" sung during Chanukah. The text is by a Jewish poet written around the 13th Century.

Ma'oz tzur y'shu-atee
L'cha na-eh l'sha-bey-ach.
Tee-kon bet t'fee-la-tee
V'sham to-dah n'za-bey-ach.
L'et ta-chin mat-bey-ach,
Mee-tzar ham'na bey-ach.
Az eg-mor b'shir miz mor
Chanukah hamiz bey-ach,
Az eg-mor b'shir miz mor
Chanukah hamiz bey-ach.

Rock of ages let our song
Praise Thy saving power.
Thou admidst the raging foes
Wast our sheltering tower.
Furious they assailed us,
But Thine arm availed us.
And Thy word broke their sword
When our own strength failed us,
And Thy word broke their sword
When our own strength failed us.

Ma'oz Tsur
Rock of Ages

Majestically

Traditional

Mi Y'Malel

Folk harpers: the levers on the F and G above middle C will have to be changed as noted in the music. You may find it easiest to play the final two notes in the bass clef with the right hand (rh), so you can change your levers.

Pedal harpists: follow the pedal changes as marked in the music.

Moderately

Traditional

This song is sometimes sung as a "round" , with the 2nd part starting after 2 measures. It celebrates the victory of the Maccabees over the Syrian king, Antiochus, in 165 B.C.E. "Macabees" is a Hebrew word the Jewish soldiers were called meaning Hammer.

Mi Y'malel g'vurot Yisrael?	Who can retell the things that befell us?
Otan mi yimne?	Who can count them?
Hen b'chol dor yakum hagibor	In every age, a hero or sage
Goel ha'am.	Came to our aid.
Sh'ma! Bayamin hahem bazman hazeh,	Hark! In days of yore, in Israel's ancient land
Maccabee moshia u'fodeh.	Brave Maccabeus led the faithful band.
Uv-yameynu kol am Yisrael	But now all Israel must as one arise,
Yitached, yakum, l'higa-el.	Redeem itself thru deed and sacrifice.

Mi Y'Malel

Folk harpers: the levers on the F and G above middle C will have to be changed as noted in the music. You may find it easiest to play the final two notes in the bass clef with the right hand (rh), so you can change your levers.
Pedal harpists: follow the pedal changes as marked in the music.

Moderately

Traditional

Ner Li

Sweetly

Traditional

A children's song about a candle used to light the menorah.

Ner li, ner li, ner li da-kik,
Ba-Chanukah neri ad-lik.
Ba-Chanukah neri ya-ir
Ba-Chanukah shirim a-shir,
Ba-Chanukah neri ya-ir
Ba-Chanukah shirim a-shir.

I have a little candle, my candle burns bright.
I light my little candle on Chanukah night.
My little candle seems to say
Thank you O God for this holiday,
My little candle seems to say
Thank you O God for this holiday.

Ner Li

Sweetly

Traditional

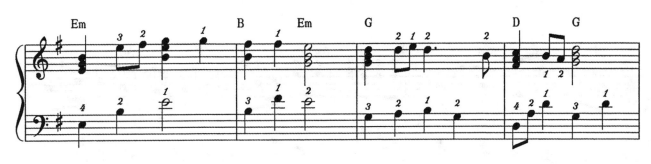

Sevivon

Folk harpers: set the G#s right above and below middle C before you begin. They will not need to be changed during the piece.
Pedal harpists: set your G pedal to G#, and you will not need to change it during the piece.

Lively   Traditional

There are many children's songs about dreydls. So often is the dreydl identified with Chanukah that it is frequently used as a symbol for the holiday. On each side of the dreydl is a hebrew letter. The letters stand for the words "Nes Gadol Haya Sham", which means "A Great Miracle Happened There" recalling the victory of the Macabees in 165 B.C.E., and the miracle of a one day's supply of oil which lasted for eight.

Sevivon sov, sov, sov,
Chanukah hu chag tov!
Chanukah hu chag tov,
Sevivon sov, sov, sov!
Chag simcha hu la-am,
Nes gadol haya-sham!
Nes gadol haya-sham,
Chag simcha hu la-am!

Little dreydl spin, spin, spin... Chanukah is a day of joy. 'A great miracle happened there.' Spin little dreydl, spin, spin, spin....

Sevivon

Folk harpers: set the G#s above and below middle C before you begin. They will not need to be changed during the piece.
Pedal harpists: set your G pedal to G#, and you will not need to change it during the piece.

Lively

Traditional

Yodim Atem

Moderately

Traditional

1. Li avi hid-lik nerot
V'shmash lo ah-vu-kah,
V'shmash lo ah-vu-kah.
Yodim atem lich-vod ma
Yodim atem lich-vod ma
Yodim atem lich-vod ma
Lich-vod ha Chanukah.

2. Li imi natna l'viva,
L'viva chama umi-tu-kah,
L'viva chama umi-tu-kah.
Yodim atem lich-vod ma
Yodim atem lich-vod ma
Yodim atem lich-vod ma
Lich-vod ha Chanukah.

1. Father lights the Chanukah candles
The shamash burns so bright,
The shamash burns so bright.
Do you know why he lights them?
Yes I know why he lights them.
Do you know why he lights them?
Because it's Chanukah.

2. Mother bakes the potato latkes,
Latkes so warm and sweet,
Latkes so warm and sweet.
Do you know why she bakes them?
Yes I know why she bakes them.
Do you know why she bakes them?
Because it's Chanukah.

Yodim Atem

Moderately

Traditional

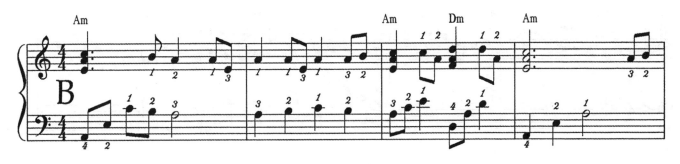

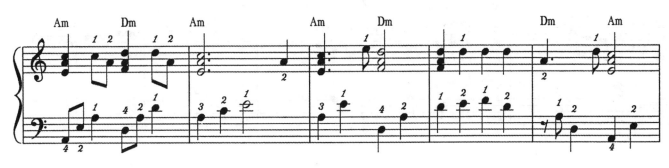

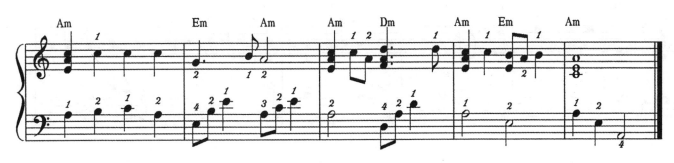

Hatikvah

Slowly

Words by N.H. Imber

This song is thought of as the official anthem of Israel. Hatikvah (The Hope) was written by a European Jewish poet during the late 1800s and the melody adapted from an old folk tune. The words were changed after the State of Israel was officially founded.

Kol od bah-le-vav p'nee-mah
Ne-fesh y'hu-dee ho-mee-ya.
U'la-fa-ah-tey miz-rach kah-dee-ma
Ah-yin l'tzee-on tzo-fee-ya.
Od lo av-dah tik-vah-tey-nu
Ha-tik-vah sh'note ahl-pa-yim,
Lih-vot am chaf-shee b'ar-tzay-nu
Eh-retz tzee-on vi-ru-sha-la-yim.

So long as a Jewish soul lives within a heart,
And his eye is turned to the East towards Zion,
Then the hope is not lost.
The hope of two thousand years that we may be
A free people in the land of Zion and Jerusalem....

Hatikvah

Folk harpers: set the D# right above middle C before you begin. It will not need to be changed during the piece.
Pedal harpists: you will need to make several D pedal changes throughout the piece.

Slowly

Words by N.H. Imber

Other Books by Sylvia Woods

Music Theory And Arranging Techniques For Folk Harps
Hymns And Wedding Music For All Harps
Teach Yourself To Play The Folk Harp
Lennon and McCartney for the Harp
50 Christmas Carols For All Harps
40 O'Carolan Tunes For All Harps
Irish Dance Tunes For All Harps
52 Scottish Songs For All Harps
50 Irish Melodies For The Harp
76 Disney Songs For The Harp
Jesu, Joy Of Man's Desiring
The Harp Of Brandiswhiere
John Denver Love Songs
Andrew Lloyd Webber
Beauty And The Beast
Pachelbel's Canon
Songs of the Harp

If you would like to receive a free catalog of books by Sylvia Woods and other books, recordings, harps, and accessories, please write to: Sylvia Woods Harp Center, P.O. Box 816, Montrose, CA 91021 USA

You can also find us on the Internet at www.harpcenter.com

CHANUKAH MUSIC
FOR ALL HARPS

by SYLVIA WOODS

This is the fourth book in the SYLVIA WOODS MULTI-LEVEL HARP BOOKS SERIES: books designed to be used by harpers and harpists of all levels of proficiency. Each tune has two arrangements: an easy version (A), and one that is more difficult (B). Also, each version contains chord indications that can be used by harp players or other instrumentalists.

Harp players can use this book many ways, depending on their purposes and abilitites. Here are a few suggestions.

1. A beginning player can play the melody alone, or with chords, or the complete easier arrangement.

2. More advanced players can play the easier arrangement, filling it out with more chords in the right or left hand, or play the second arrangement.

3. The easy arrangement can be played first, and then the harder arrangement, making a varied set.

4. The two arrangements can be played as a duet.

5. Additional instruments can be added to either arrangement, playing either the chords or the melody.

We hope you enjoy this book. If you'd like information on other books in this series, and other books by Sylvia Woods, please write to the Sylvia Woods Harp Center, P.O. Box 816, Montrose, CA 91021 USA and request our free mail order catalog.

ALPHABETICAL INDEX OF TUNES

6 69619 66108 0

ISBN 0-936661-08-9

DISTRIBUTED BY HAL LEONARD

0 73999 60220 3

00660220   U.S. $9.95